IRAN: A WRIT OF DECEPTION AND COVER-UP

IRANIAN REGIME'S SECRET COMMITTEE HID MILITARY DIMENSIONS OF ITS NUCLEAR PROGRAM

NATIONAL COUNCIL OF RESISTANCE OF IRAN
US REPRESENTATIVE OFFICE

1747 Pennsylvania Ave., NW, Suite 1125, Washington, DC 20006;
Tel: 202-747-7847; Fax 202-330-5346; info@ncrius.org; twitter: @ncrius

DECEMBER 1, 2015

IRAN: A WRIT OF DECEPTION AND COVER-UP; Iranian Regime's Secret Committee Hid Military Dimensions of its Nuclear Program

First published in 2016 by

National Council of Resistance of Iran - U.S. Representative Office (NCRI-US), 1747 Pennsylvania Ave., NW, Suite 1125, Washington, DC 20006

ISBN-13: 978-0-9904327-4-6

ISBN-10: 0-9904327-4-2

Library of Congress Cataloging-in-Publication Data

National Council of Resistance of Iran - U.S. Representative Office.

IRAN: A WRIT OF DECEPTION AND COVER-UP; Iranian Regime's Secret Committee Hid Military Dimensions of its Nuclear Program

1. Iran-Military policy.   2. Nuclear weapons-Iran.   3. Iran-Foreign relations.
4. Security, International.   5. Rouhani, Hassan.

First Edition: January 2016

Printed in the United States of America

Table of Contents

Supreme Leader Ali Khamenei
visits Imam Hussein University

Executive Summary

Based on reliable information obtained by the Mujahedin-e Khalq (MEK) network inside Iran, a top-secret committee is in charge of drafting the answers to the International Atomic Energy Agency (IAEA) regarding the Possible Military Dimensions (PMD) of Tehran's nuclear program.

Top officials from the Islamic Revolutionary Guards Corps (IRGC) and the Ministry of Defense Armed Forces Logistics (MODAFL) comprise the committee's key members. They have been tasked with drafting the responses to IAEA's PMD inquiries working to cover up the military dimensions, thus resolving and terminating the PMD dispute by forging suitable scenarios for non-military usage of the program, which would seem plausible to the IAEA, and to falsely convince the international community that Iran has never been after the nuclear bomb.

This committee prepared the PMD answers delivered to the IAEA on August 15, 2015.

Among the foremost issues related to the PMD question are the explosive detonators called EBW (Exploding Bridge Wire) detonator, which is an integral part of a program to develop an implosion type nuclear device.

In its September 2014 report, IAEA stated that Iran has offered "information and explanations to the Agency on Iran's work after 2007 related to the application of EBW detonators in the oil and gas industry which was not inconsistent with specialized industry practices."

Tehran forged documents and exchanged communication between the Oil Ministry and the Defense Ministry to prove that the EBWs were produced and used by the oil industry.

But according to an exhaustive investigation by the Iranian Resistance involving dozens of sources, the National Iranian Drilling Company (NIDC), which is responsible for all oil and gas drilling, has not received even one of EBW detonators that had been produced by the Ministry of Defense. The information contained in this book renders the regime's claims utterly false.

Activities of the Committee
to Deceive IAEA on PMD Probe

Image © 2015 DigitalGlobe

➢ Held regular meetings from July until October 2015 to prepare PMD response

➢ Meetings held at the Defense Ministry's Intern'l Affairs Directorate, located at the Defense Ministry's headquarters in north Tehran on Langari Street.

Information Details

The final disposition of the true nature of Tehran's nuclear program was one of the major disputes between world community and the Iranian regime. In order to determine the true nature of this program or its Possible Military Dimensions (PMD), the International Atomic Energy Agency (IAEA) identified certain items in November 2011 to which the clerical regime had to respond. Following the nuclear agreement in July 2015, Tehran pledged again that it would fully answer the questions.

Meanwhile, Tehran sought to receive confirmation on the peaceful nature of its nuclear program and prove its long-standing claim in this regard by terminating this case.

The Mujahedin-e Khalq (MEK) network inside Iran has obtained reliable information that a top-secret committee is in charge of drafting the answers to IAEA regarding the PMD with the intention to deceive the UN nuclear watchdog.

Top officials from the Islamic Revolutionary Guards Corps (IRGC) and the Ministry of Defense Armed Forces Logistics (MODAFL) comprise the key members of this committee. They are tasked with drafting the preliminary and final answers to IAEA's PMD inquiries.

In light of their deep knowledge of the military dimensions of the program, the committee members are working to cover up the military dimensions, thus resolving and terminating the PMD dispute by forging suitable scenarios for non-military usage of the program, which would seem plausible to the IAEA.

The committee is tasked with finalizing the answers and provides them to the Atomic Energy Organization of Iran (AEOI) to be passed onto the IAEA by the AEOI's safeguards affairs department, an agency that is officially accountable to the IAEA inspectors in Iran.

The information collected and examined by the Iranian Resistance since July until late October from sources within the IRGC, MODAFEL, Organization of Defensive Innovation and Research (SPND), and the AEOI, identifies five members of this secret committee.[1]

Make-up of Committee for Drafting Answers to IAEA

The three main individuals in charge of preparing and drafting the PMD answers to the IAEA are:

1. Brigadier General Nasrollah Kalantari, deputy Defense Minister;

2. Seyed Ahmad Mirzaei, general director for disarmament at the Ministry of Defense;

3. Mohsen Fakhrizadeh Mahabadi, head of the Organization of Defensive Innovation and Research (SPND).

Two officials from the Counter-Intelligence Dept. of the Defense Ministry who cooperate with Nasrollah Kalantari are Hedayati and Moussavi.

The most senior official in this committee is Nasrollah Kalantari, deputy Defense Minister, but all the answers and reports prepared in response to IAEA questions on PMD were confirmed and signed by Mohsen Fakhrizadeh as the official directly in charge of the nuclear weapons program.

---

[1]SPND stands for the Farsi acronym of *Sazemane Pazhouheshhaye Novine Defaeei*. This organization, formed in February 2011, is the agency in charge of weaponizing the nuclear project, and was first revealed by the MEK in July 2011, and was designated by the Treasury Department in August 2014.
See: http://usatoday30.usatoday.com/news/washington/2011-07-23-iran-nuclear-program_n.htm
http://www.state.gov/r/pa/prs/ps/2014/231159.htm

Brigadier General Nasrollah Kalantari *(left)*
The most senior official in this committee

Background on committee members:

Members of the committee are veteran IRGC commanders who have been involved in the 30-year process of building the Iranian regime's nuclear weapons program. Mohsen Fakhrizadeh and Seyed Ahmad Mirzaei, in particular, are key IRGC officers who began their activities three decades ago at the IRGC research center by working on weapons of mass destruction (WMD), i.e., nuclear, biological and chemical, and have been involved in the regime's nuclear weapons and WMD projects throughout the years.

Procedure for drafting answers to PMD questions

Mohsen Fakhrizadeh follows up on the details of drafting the answers with the help of a team of SPND staff and experts. They are tasked with drafting a suitable answer for every subject included in the PMD questions. The committee subsequently examines those answers and Fakhrizadeh makes the final confirmation before they are passed to the IAEA.

This team held regular meetings from July until October to answer the PMD questions. The meetings were held at the Defense Ministry's International Affairs Directorate, located at the Defense Ministry's headquarters in north Tehran on Langari Street.

This committee prepared the answers delivered to the IAEA on August 15, 2015.

Mohsen Fakhrizadeh Mahabadi and Ahmad Mirzaei were especially sensitive to IAEA's inspections of military sites and declared their strong opposition to direct inspections. This committee devised the plan and outlines of inspections of military centers and crafted various rules and regulations to restrict IAEA inspectors under the pretext of safeguarding military secrets.

The committee also decided to ban IAEA inspectors from conducting interviews with key officials and experts involved in the nuclear program. If any interviews are to take place, they must be conducted from behind the curtains or in writing. The excuse is to prevent the regime's scientists from being identified for the fear of their own safety and security. Such arrangements obviously enable the regime to advance its pre-meditated scenarios.

Background information on key figures

IRGC Brigadier General Nasrollah Kalantari:

He has served as the Defense Ministry's Deputy for International Affairs, Communications and Defense Studies since 2010. He plays a significant role in devising the regime's macro policies on military affairs. He has worked for years in the Defense Ministry's research and studies affairs and is the senior official in the three-member decision-making committee on PMD. As deputy Minister of Defense Brigadier General Nasrollah Kalantari travelled to Armenia in 2013 and to China in October 2015.

Brigadier General Nasrollah Kalantari

Mohsen Fakhrizadeh Mahabadi:

Fakhrizadeh is presently the head of the Organization of Defensive Innovation and Research (SPND) and is one of the deputies in the Defense Ministry.

Mohsen Fakhrizadeh Mahabadi

Since the revolution in 1979, Fakhrizadeh became a member of the IRGC. He had studied nuclear engineering and started working at the IRGC research center. He became a member of the scientific board of the School of Physics at IRGC Imam Hussein University since 1991. He succeeded Seyyed Abbas Shahmoradi as head of the Physics

Research Center also known as Institute of Applied Physics, which was the former name of this agency in charge of making nuclear weapons. The initial team in charge of making nuclear weapons was known as the Fakhrizadeh Team.

Fakhrizadeh's alias name within the regime is Dr. Hassan Mohseni. Hassan is the name of his father and Mohsen is his first name turned into surname.

The National Council of Resistance of Iran first disclosed the name of Mohsen Fakhrizadeh in November 2004 as head of the agency making the nuclear weapon. Fakhrizadeh was designated in UNSCR 1747 (2007) and by the United States in July 2008 for his involvement in Iran's proscribed WMD activities. The IAEA has been requesting to interview Fakhrizadeh for years, a request the regime has so far refused.

Fakhrizadeh's signature can be seen on the various documents related to PMD available with the IAEA, as the highest official directly in charge of the agency making nuclear weapons at the Ministry of Defense.

Seyed Ahmad Mirzaei:

Seyed Ahmad Mirzaei is one of the regime's first experts on biological weapons at the IRGC research center. He has been involved in this field since the Iran-Iraq war. He is considered one of the regime's top experts on WMD. The Iranian Resistance exposed his name in February 2008 as one of the highest officials associated with the nuclear weapons manufacturing agency headed by Mohsen Fakhrizadeh Mahabadi. He has regularly had a close relationship with Mohsen Fakhrizadeh Mahabadi. His official position in recent years has been director general of the Defense Ministry's Disarmament Department. From 2004 to 2005, he followed up the IAEA inspections of military sites like Haft-e Tir and Parchin on behalf of the Ministry of Defense.

Other decision-making agencies on PMD:

In addition to the team based at the Defense Ministry's International Directorate whose task is to prepare the technical part of the answers, there are a series of agencies involved in making the political and executive decisions.

A. <u>Supreme Leader, Ali Khamenei and his personal advisors</u>: Khamenei personally finalizes decisions on nuclear affairs. Some officials of Khamenei's office, including former Foreign Minister, Ali Akbar Velayati, have significant input on the final decisions.

Ali Khamenei

B. <u>Deputy on Strategic Affairs of the Supreme National Security Council</u>: This position is presently held by IRGC Brigadier General Ali Hossein Tash, one of the most senior officials who has been pursuing the regime's nuclear weapons program. For years, as acting Minister of Defense, he oversaw the progress of Fakhrizadeh's plans. The Supreme National Security Council holds the main expert meetings for making decisions on nuclear issues. Brig. Gen. Hossein Tash, on behalf of the SNSC, oversees the work of the main committee answering PMD questions.

Ali Akbar Velayati

Brigadier General Ali Hossein Tash

A. Atomic Energy Organization's Safeguards Affairs: This is the unit directly accountable to IAEA inspectors in Iran. Presently, it is headed by Amini, general director for Safety and Safeguards Affairs, and his deputy is Pejman Rahimian who handles all matters involving the inspectors.

B. Relevant Foreign Ministry agencies

A case study of regime's duplicity in responding to IAEA inquiries

Among the foremost issues related to the PMD question are the explosive detonators called EBW (Exploding Bridge Wire) detonator that has been pursued by the International Atomic Energy Agency since 2005.[2]

The development of safe, fast-acting detonators, such as EBWs, and equipment suitable for firing the detonators, is an integral part of a program to develop an implosion type nuclear device.

an integral part of a program to develop an implosion type nuclear device.

The aforementioned team fabricated a scenario to address this issue and eventually in April-May 2014 presented regime's response to the IAEA. A study of this case offers a very good example about the scope of deception employed by the Iranian regime in working with the IAEA.

---

[2] These EBW detonators are also called Electrical Bridge Wire detonators.

Outfit to respond to PMD inquiry

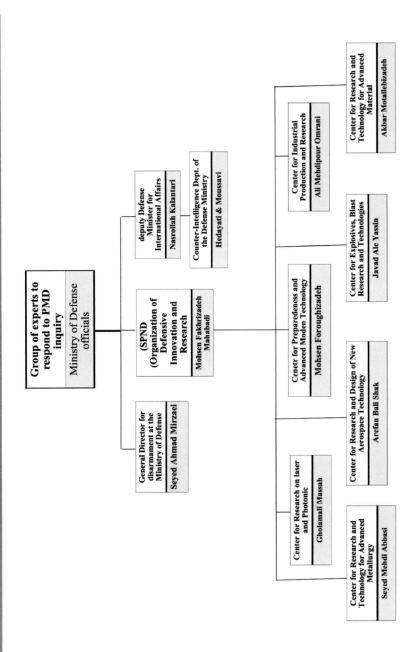

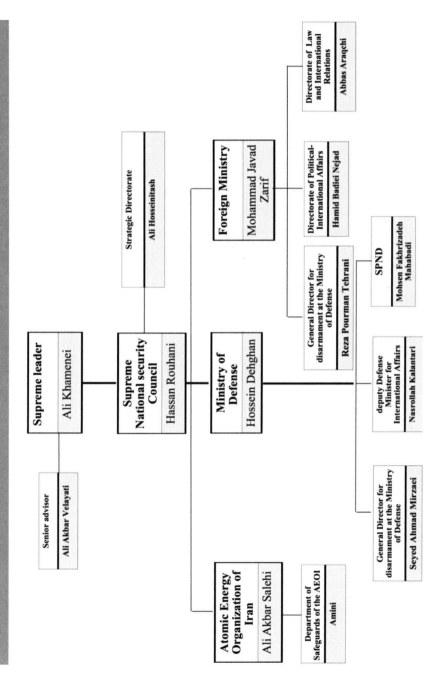

Entities Involved in decision making on response to IAEA

This is the same subject that Abbas Araqchi (deputy foreign minister) discussed with the directors of regime's radio and television (IRIB). That interview was supposed to have been confidential but was inadvertently posted on regime's radio and television website. This posting on August 1, 2015 that was promptly removed stated: "[Western countries]

Abbas Araqchi

turned Iran's file that was entirely technical into a political issue dubbed PMD and thus they were constantly working with the IAEA feeding this agency additional information that made matters worse. It was so that the EBW (explosive detonator) was revealed. You can ask the friends at the Ministry of Defense, they are very troubled by the leakage of information that aggravated the situation."

Background on IAEA raising the issue of EBW detonators

According to the IAEA February 2006 report, the documents related to military nuclear activities, including the activities related to high explosives, were first raised with the regime on December 5, 2005, but the regime refused to respond and stated that the allegations "are based on false and fabricated documents so they were baseless." This matter continued as a point of dispute between the regime and the IAEA for eight years.

The annex to the IAEA's November 2011 report discusses in detail the regime's military nuclear activities in 12 areas. Four of the 12 PMD issues are related to this type of detonators.

Ultimately, in February 2014, the regime reached an agreement with the IAEA to address seven of those areas, including the EBW detonators. According to the IAEA report on June 2014, the regime presented documents and explanations to the IAEA in April and May 2014.

Regime claims these detonators are used in oil and gas industries

In its report of September 2014, IAEA eventually stated that the Iranian regime has offered some explanations about its decision to expand the work on safe detonators in early 2000 plus "information and explanations to the Agency on Iran's work after 2007 related to the application of EBW detonators in the oil and gas industry which was not inconsistent with specialized industry practices."[3]

The regime argued that replicating these detonators had been for non-military purposes and specifically for the oil and gas industry.

The IAEA Director General is quoted in the September 2014 report as saying: "the Director General further noted that the Agency would need to consider all past outstanding issues, including EBW detonators, integrating all of them in a 'system' and addressing the 'system' as a whole."[4]

EBW not used in Iran's oil and gas industry

According to an exhaustive investigation by the Iranian Resistance involving dozens of sources, the National Iranian Drilling Company (NIDC), which is responsible for drilling oil and gas, has not received even one of EBW detonators that had been produced by the Ministry of Defense. This renders the regime's claims utterly false.

While the oil and gas industry experts who work on the wells are at risk and regime's officials are fully aware of this matter, no EBW detonator has been used in this industry.

---

[3] https://www.iaea.org/sites/default/files/gov2014-43.pdf
[4] ibid

An internal report by the National Iranian Oil Company (NIOC) sent to the Oil Ministry's Inspector General from the Special Drilling Services section in August 2015 reads: "Although it is around two years that we have requested safe detonators of type EBW from the Ministry of Defense, we have not received even one of these detonators. Failing to respond to this matter endangers the lives of the engineers and technicians of this section. For example, last year, when we had to check the condition of a well in Kish Island, we were forced to use unsafe detonators by accepting to risk the lives of these people. Please act urgently in this regard." In another part of this report, it is suggested that more advanced detonators called DYNAWELL RF-Safe Electronic Detonator be purchased from DYNAWELL Company in Germany.

At the NIDC, the Special Drilling Services Section is responsible for the activities relating to the usage of explosive material for gas and oil wells. The General Director of this section is currently an engineer named Ali Daqayeqi that was appointed to this position in 2014. Other directors working in the Special Drilling Services are: Mohammad Farzad Hemmatian, director of logging section, Dr. Afshin Makvandi, director of supplies, and Talebzadeh head of the procurement department.

In requesting flammable material from the Ministry of Defense, Hossein Sharifi responsible for the explosive material at NIDC, is in contact with Soltani, the director of marketing department of Sattari Industry, affiliated with the munition industry.

The Special Drilling Service has specific links with the Ministry of Defense and has been receiving detonators and conventional explosive material from the Ministry of Defense.

Inside the Ministry of Defense, Sattari Industry and Parsian Technology are the two companies, which supply the Oil Ministry with detonators and explosive materials and they have not given EBW detonators to the NIDC.

Regime's deception scheme in dealing with IAEA inquiry

The scenario to respond to the IAEA inquiry has been put together by a committee from the Ministry of Defense to make it appear as though the Oil Ministry had placed a request for EBW detonators. IAEA was provided with this response in April-May 2014.

According to this scheme whose details were completed in the past year, the regime's scenario and the steps used by the regime to make it work are as the following:

A. Since early 2000, the Oil Ministry has been raising the problem with explosions and the casualties of oil wells with the Ministry of Defense. Thus, the Ministry of Defense decided to develop its safe detonators.

B. Subsequently, a series of written exchanges were prepared between these two ministries and passed on to the IAEA to prove that the Oil Ministry had made the requests.

C. A series of videos were shown to the IAEA inspectors, which showed activities by the regime in testing these detonators.

D. A collection of documents on the use of these detonators in other industries was shown to prove that they are not exclusively used for nuclear military purposes.

E. A series of reports and internal communications prepared by the regime purport that this type of detonators had been used in the oil industry since 2007.

F. Attempts were made to rebut IAEA documents that specifically showed research on this type of detonators had been conducted in relation to the Physics Research Center (former entity in charge of building the nuclear weapon).

Deception scheme in dealing with IAEA inquiries

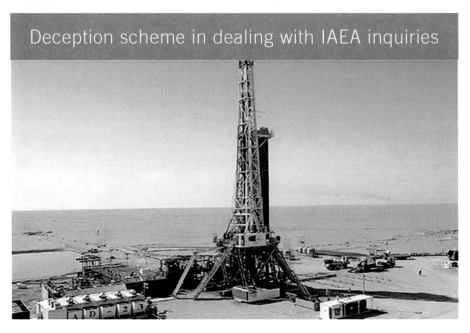

➢ Iran told IAEA in April-May 2014 that Oil Ministry requested these EBW detonators for drilling purposes.

➢ Iran took 6 steps to sell its story to the IAEA.

Iran took 6 steps to sell its story to the IAEA

1. Fabricated the story that since early 2000, the Oil Ministry has been raising the problem with explosions and the casualties of oil wells with the Ministry of Defense, which decided to develop its safe EBW detonators.

2. Subsequently, a series of written exchanges were prepared between these two ministries and passed on to the IAEA to prove that the Oil Ministry had made the requests.

3. A series of videos were shown to the IAEA inspectors, which showed activities by the regime in testing these detonators.

4. A collection of documents on the use of these detonators in other industries was shown to prove that they are not exclusively used for nuclear military purposes.

5. A series of reports and internal communications prepared by the regime purport that this type of detonators had been used in the oil industry since 2007.

6. Attempts were made to rebut IAEA documents that specifically showed research on this type of detonators had been conducted in relation to the Physics Research Center (former entity in charge of building the nuclear weapon).

Exposing the agency and experts that worked on developing EBW detonators

The agency that works on the production of highly explosive material used as the detonator for the nuclear bomb is the Center for Explosives, Blast Research and Technologies (METFAZ), which is one of the seven subsections of the Organization of Defensive Innovation and Research (SPND) that is headed by Mohsen Fakhrizadeh Mahabadi.[5]

IRGC official Saeed Borji who has been the head of METFAZ for a long time plays a key role in the tests referred to by the IAEA.

METFAZ has its headquarters in Tehran Pars District of Tehran with several branches in Tehran and its vicinity. The head of the METFAZ is currently an engineer named Javad Ale Yassin, an IRGC veteran.

The main site for the activities of this organ is located in a collection of underground tunnels in southeastern Tehran in the general district of Khojir towards Parchin near Sanjarian village; 10 kilometers along Babaii Hwy towards Parchin. Details of the pictures and the location of this site were disclosed by the Iranian Resistance in September 2009.

METFAZ uses Parchin site to conduct its tests on explosives.

Main site for the activities of METFAZ is in underground tunnels in southeast Tehran in the general district of Khojir

---

[5] The Farsi acronym is *Markaze Tahghighat va Tose'he Fanavari Enfejar va Zarbeh*

Parchin

METFAZ uses Parchin site to conduct its tests on explosives.

Center for Research and Technology for Advanced Material – Chemical Group

In addition to METFAZ, the Center for Research and Technology for Advanced Material – Chemical Group is another section of SPND that works in connection with the above tests.

In the new arrangement of SPND, this group is known as the Karimi Group and the previous name of this center was Center for Research and Technology for Advanced Material – Chemical Group (Farsi acronym-METSHAN). An engineer called Akbar Motallebizadeh heads this group. This center has worked on advanced chemical material used in building warheads and missiles. Headquarter of METSHAN is located in Mojdeh Street where the original SPND headquarters was located.

Summary and Conclusion:

The key individuals involved in forging explanations regarding the PMD issue for the IAEA are the same individuals who have themselves been key in the production of nuclear weapon during the past years and their responses were prepared with the objective to cover up the military dimensions of the nuclear project and to falsely convince the international community that Iran has never been after the nuclear bomb.

In particular, concerning the development of EBW detonators, an integral part of a program to develop an implosion type nuclear device, the Iranian regime's claim that these detonators are needed for the oil industry is a sheer lie and was provided to the IAEA with the objective of diverting IAEA investigations.

Appendix

Notable Nuclear Revelations of the Iranian Resistance (1991-2015)

Since 1991 the Iranian resistance has exposed more than a 100 secret nuclear projects of the Iranian regime. Some of the more notable nuclear revelations include:

➤ Revealing the regime's preliminary nuclear facilities in Mo'alm Kalaye (1991);

➤ Revealing the attempt to purchase nuclear warheads from Kazakhstan (1992), the revelation aborted the shipment of the warheads to Iran;

➤ Continuous revelation of hiring Chinese, Russian and N. Korean experts and the regime's teams travelling to these countries over the years on dozens of occasions;

➤ Revealing the uranium enrichment facility in Natanz, being the largest and most expansive of the regime's investment on its nuclear weapons program. The site was exposed on August 14, 2002 in Washington, DC, and disrupted Tehran's nuclear calculations and led IAEA inspections to Iran that confirmed the revelation;

➤ Revealing the heavy water project in Arak (August 14, 2002) in a press conference in Washington, DC;

➤ Revealing the most important companies involved in producing and importing equipment and necessary material for nuclear projects (February 2003 and August-September 2013), including Kala Electric in Aab-Ali highway that was registered as a watch-making factory. However, this was actually a center for centrifuge assembly and testing, and in an IAEA inspection, traces of highly enriched uranium was found at this site;

➤ Revealing the Lavizan-Shian Center (May 2003). This was a very sensitive nuclear site for the regime and the mullahs immediately destroyed it and even removed the soil before allowing a June 2004 IAEA visit to the site;

➤ Revealing the Lashkarabad site and its front company (May 2003). This site was inspected by the IAEA (October 2003), and the regime deceived the inspectors by taking them to another location;

➤ Revealing in November 2003, the special role of the IRGC in the nuclear projects clearly showed the military goals and aspects of this project;

➤ In April 2004, the NCRI revealed that Tehran had dedicated 400 nuclear experts to military industries;

➤ Exposing the new Center for Readiness and New Defense Technology (Lavizan-2) in April 2004. The equipment and activities from razed Lavizan site was moved to this site, but the site was kept off limits;

➤ In September 2004, NCRI revealed the allotment of $16bn to nuclear technology, purchase and smuggling of Deuterium from Russia, as well as details on the AEOI's companies;

➤ Revealing the Hemmat Missile Industries site in relation to produce nuclear chemical warheads (December 2004);

➤ Revealing a project in February 2005 aimed at producing polonium-210 and beryllium to build nuclear bomb fuses;

➤ Revealing the secret nuclear center in the Parchin tunnel (March 2005). This site focused on laser enrichment;

➤ Revealing the production and importing graphite necessary for nuclear bomb production (May 2005);

➤ Revealing the import and production of Maraging steel to build the bomb fuselage and using it in centrifuge systems (July 2005);

➤ Revealing the production of 4,000 ready-to-install centrifuges (August 2005);

➤ Revealing in a press conference in Washington, DC, in August 2005, the meeting between Abdul Qadeer Khan, and commanders of the Iranian Revolutionary Guards in 1986 and 1987 in Tehran;

➤ Revealing in Brussels the regime's plans to smuggle tritium from South Korea to increase nuclear explosion power (September 2005);

➤ Revealing, in a Washington, DC, press conference, the regime's tunnel construction in its military centers to keep secret the material and equipment (September 2005);

➤ In a Washington, DC, press conference in November 2005, NCRI revealed that Iran was building nuclear capable missiles in underground secret tunnels;

➤ Revealing the construction of an underground site near Qom (Fordow) in December 2005;

➤ Revealing importing of industrial press machines to shape enriched uranium in a bomb (January 2006);

➤ Revealing the production of P2 centrifuges (August 2006);

➤ Revealing in Washington, DC, the reactivation of laser enrichment projects (September 2006);

➤ Revealing the specifications of 7 nuclear front companies related to the nuclear fuel cycle (February 2007);47

➤ Revealing a secret tunnel being constructed by the Ministry of Defense south of the Natanz site (September 2007);

➤ Revealing the location of nuclear warhead construction in Khojeir and the nuclear weapon command center in Mojdeh (February 2008);

- ➤ Revealing Beheshti University as a nuclear research center related to commanding weapons production in Mojdeh (March 2008);

- ➤ Revealing Center of Explosion and Impact Technology (METFAZ) and changes in the nuclear command center (September 2009);

- ➤ Revealing further details about the Fordow site (October 2009);

- ➤ In September 2010, in Washington, D.C., the NCRI revealed a covert nuclear site located in tunnels in Behjatabad in the Abyek Township of Qazvin Province. This covert nuclear site was codenamed "311" and is known as Javadinia 2;

- ➤ In April 2011, the NCRI revealed in Washington, DC, the covert site near Tehran, named TABA, which was involved in production of centrifuge parts for tens of thousands of centrifuges. Tehran conceded the existence of this site the next day;

- ➤ Revealing in Washington, DC, in July 2011, the Defensive Innovation and Research Organization (SPND) nuclear bomb command center chaired by Mohsen Fakhrizadeh. SPND was later sanctioned by the Department of State in August 2014;

- ➤ Revealing 100 names of nuclear engineering experts active in various bomb making sections (January 2012);

- ➤ Revealing in Washington, DC, further details of SPND operations, its involvement in the Fordow site, and the list of experts associated with this center (April 2012);

- ➤ Revealing the top-secret Maadan Sharq nuclear site in Tehran's Damavand district. (July 2013);

- ➤ Revealing the relocation of Defensive Innovation and Research Organization (SPND) nuclear bomb command center (October 2013);

- ➤ Revealing the "012" secret site in Isfahan's Mobarakeh linked to SPND (November 2013).

➢ In a Washington, DC conference, revealing the Iranian regime's activities related to high explosive chambers at Parchin military site (November 2014);

➢ Revealing in a press conference in Washington, DC, the existence of Lavizan-3 underground nuclear site in Tehran used for advanced centrifuge testing and research and development (February 2015).

➢ Revealing the cooperation between the Iranian regime and North Korea regarding the nuclear weapons program of Iran and the presence of North Korean nuclear scientists in Tehran (May 2015).

➢ Revealing Iran's deceitful tactics during nuclear negotiations with the P 5+1 (June 2015).

➢ Revealing Iran's cooperation with North Korea to deceive IAEA inspectors (September 2015).

➢ Revealing how Iran laid out a plan to deceive the IAEA in its probe of Possible Military Dimensions of Iran's nuclear program (December 2015).